"I was honored to read this copy of the boo.., *.. ...ve ser us Free: Scriptural Reflections for Trauma Survivors*. It makes a profound connection between Scripture, the suffering of Jesus, and the pain of trauma survivors. The associated prayers add further meaning and may help survivors find a path for healing and perhaps a way to God. The description of trauma is very helpful for laypersons or professionals working in trauma recovery."

— Mary Jane Doerr, Director
Office for the Protection of Children and Youth
Archdiocese of Chicago

"I heartily endorse Father Schmidt's reflection and encourage anyone who has experienced a major traumatic event in their life to see in this book a pathway to unite oneself with the traumatic events of Jesus' suffering, death, and resurrection. It was by those saving actions that Jesus was able to free us from the debilitating effects of traumatic, sinful, and evil actions in the world. It is my hope and prayer that by a prayerful reading of this book, trauma survivors truly will be set free to live with the Joy of Jesus' life within them."

— Bishop Paul J. Bradley
Bishop of Kalamazoo

"I found the Trauma Model very useful in helping people come in touch with their trauma by naming the trauma, processing and integrating their emotions, thoughts, and behavior. The reflections are very inspiring and touching."

— Sr. Tecla Chepng'eno, FMSJ
Section Manager
International Missionary Benefits Society (IMS),
East Africa Section

YOU HAVE SET US free

Scriptural Reflections for Trauma Survivors

Kenneth W. Schmidt

LITURGICAL PRESS
Collegeville, Minnesota

www.litpress.org

1   2   3   4   5   6   7   8   9

Library of Congress Cataloging-in-Publication Data

Names: Schmidt, Kenneth W., author.
Title: You have set us free : scriptural reflections for trauma survivors / Kenneth W. Schmidt.
Description: Collegeville, Minnesota : Liturgical Press, [2016]
Identifiers: LCCN 2016010931 (print) | LCCN 2016034202 (ebook) | ISBN 9780814647127 | ISBN 9780814647370 (ebook)
Subjects: LCSH: Psychic trauma—Patients—Religious life. | Post-traumatic stress disorder—Patients—Religious life. | Catholic Church—Prayers and devotions.
Classification: LCC BV4910.45 .S36 2016 (print) | LCC BV4910.45 (ebook) | DDC 242/.4—dc23
LC record available at https://lccn.loc.gov/2016010931

This book is dedicated to my colleague

Sharon Froom

whose experience, wisdom, and insight
are expressed throughout these pages.

It's been a joy and blessing to minister with you.

Contents

Introduction

The goal of this volume is to integrate spirituality and psychology, two realms of a human's personhood that are profound and have a major influence on how we understand ourselves, how we think, how we feel, and how we behave. The psychoeducational foundation is the Trauma Model, a paradigm for understanding and healing of childhood trauma based on the work of Dr. Colin Ross.

Trauma is an event or series of events combined with an individual's unique vulnerability that creates an obstacle in normal human development. The effects of trauma tend to be more obvious when the abuse or neglect occurs during childhood, but trauma can occur at any age. Some people suffer a series of traumas throughout their lives, and the lack of healing from earlier traumas interferes with healing of subsequent traumas regardless of when they occur.

Many people do not acknowledge the trauma in their history because they are ashamed. They believe that what happened was normal or expectable or what they deserved. Some believe that it was given to them by God or merely a coincidence. Nevertheless, they are still traumatized because of the impact on their neurological development and the interruption or adverse effects on their emotional development.

So what constitutes trauma? The event or events can be any form of abuse, be it physical, emotional, verbal, or sexual. Trauma may also be the result of severe neglect or negligence: the absence of care, protection, nurturance, and safety, or even the absence of the necessities of life including food and shelter. Abandonment, whether real or unintentional, can be traumatic: be it a parent who leaves, or a significant person who dies or who ends his or her own life, or a significant absence for a length of time, for example, due to a hospitalization or a mental illness. Natural disasters and tragedies can also be traumatic: hurricanes and tornadoes, floods and earthquakes, or vehicle accidents, house fires, or other mishaps. Being of minority status within a rejecting culture can also be traumatic: differences of culture, religion, language, ethnicity or race, sexual orientation or gender identification—anything that results in a person not feeling safe or having some sense of belonging. Medical problems can be traumatic as well, be they one's own or the issues of another significant person in one's life.

However, it is not the event alone that constitutes trauma but the event coupled with the vulnerability of the person who experiences the event. Children in the same family can respond differently to the same situation. One's age can influence how one experiences and interprets the traumatic event, as well as one's temperament. The context or time at which the event occurs can also influence its effects. If, for example, one lives in an alcoholic home, or experiences the tenuousness of life due to poverty, or witnesses the physical abuse of a sibling, there is already a sense of vulnerability in one's life, and the event may be the thing that tips the balance.

Finally, it might be helpful to consider that it's not necessary to determine whether some event "fits the definition" of trauma. People experience the effects of traumas as a continuum, a range of symptoms and consequences, rather than drawing a hard-and-fast conclusion that "it is" or "it isn't."

The Trauma Model

The major premise of the Trauma Model is that healing occurs at the level of naming, processing, and integrating one's emotions, thoughts, and behaviors. The goal is to help individuals improve their functioning by helping them learn tools to stabilize their internal world (their thinking and feeling) and external world (their actions, and the situations in which they live). This model helps trauma survivors identify conflicts and unlearn specific distortions related to the effects of the trauma. The model focuses on exercises that foster the development of self-awareness and processing the trauma on a feeling level with an emphasis on regulating those feelings.

The model also teaches the importance of learning about the effects of trauma and why they are long lasting. Many people assume that the effects of the trauma simply disappear with the passage of time, but that is not the case. The memories have been formed neurobiologically and they are retained by the brain whether they are conscious or not.

A person can be "triggered" by any person, object, sound, taste, smell, or reminder of the trauma, and then reacts based on the filter of one's trauma history rather than the reality of the current situation. In fact, we know from research that memory recall is unreliable, at best, and trauma memories can be skewed by the emotions attached to those memories. Healing does not take place by recalling or reliving memories, but by learning new healthy skills related to one's feelings, thinking, and behaving in the present.

Signs of Unresolved Trauma

Inability to tolerate feelings or conflicts:

- Blunt feelings or numbness, withdrawal, no obvious affect in appropriate situations
- Movement to intense or overwhelming feelings suddenly and rapidly (e.g., rage)
- Depression (problem sleeping, eating, poor energy, low motivation, poor self esteem, poor memory, anxiety)

- Panic feelings (trouble breathing, feeling as if having a heart attack, fearful, anxious, etc.)

A pattern of out-of-control and self-injurious behavior:

- Addictive behaviors (over/under-eating, gambling, drinking, smoking, etc.)
- Patterns of repeated behavior to avoid feelings (promiscuity, internet use, sleeping, etc.)
- Chaos in life (problems with relationships, employment, finances, etc.)
- Self-harmful behavior (often "alluded to" but not obvious such as scratching and cutting, nail biting, burning self, hair pulling, etc.)

Intense self-blame and feelings of unworthiness or belief they are "ruined":

- Belief that they were responsible for original trauma
- Irrational/illogical beliefs about responsibility for events in the present
- Belief that they are bad, a failure, unlovable, a loser, damaged, insignificant, worthless
- May induce others to treat them badly

Staying stuck in the victim, perpetrator, or rescuer roles:

- Seek out relationships with abusive people
- Induce abuse from others rather than waiting for it to happen
- Perceive abuse which confirms the belief that they are unworthy and unlovable
- Hurt others (different than appropriate self-protection)
- Act aggressively toward others who are weak and vulnerable

- Compulsively driven to help others, often to their own detriment
- Acts of generosity not in accord with the relationship

Disorganized attachment patterns:
- Inability to tolerate their ambivalence toward the perpetrator even after the trauma ceases
- Inability to tolerate their ambivalence toward other trusted figures, such as failed rescuers or those who denied the trauma
- Inability to tolerate their ambivalence toward significant persons currently in their lives

Difficulty maintaining healthy relationships:
- Avoid relationships altogether
- Avoid close relationships because of inherent risk
- Avoid situations that might lead to closeness
- Protect themselves, e.g., unfriendly to others before others are unfriendly to them
- Have intense but brief relationships
- Remain attached even when the relationship is unhealthy
- Perceive the relationship in a distorted manner

Black and white thinking and other cognitive distortions:
- Child-like, concrete, and magical thinking
- What they think is normal and real does not coincide with "real life"
- Derive "life rules" and "automatic thoughts" from childhood distortions
- Cling to the distortions despite challenge or contrary evidence

- Provoke a non-existent reality into being in order to verify a distortion
- Collect evidence to support the distortion while ignoring evidence to the contrary
- Patterns of distorted thinking (such as generalizations, all or nothing, discounting, jumping to conclusions, assuming, labeling, and emotional reasoning)

Intrusive thoughts, images, feelings, memories, and nightmares about the trauma

Pathological dissociation:

- Loss of (long) spaces of time (can't remember what they said or did)
- Appear to "switch" personalities, or be different people, even in speech and behavior
- Trances or sleepwalking
- Childhood companions, "voices," "too much noise in my head"
- Inability to recall important information, usually of a stressful or traumatic nature
- Confusion about personal identity or assumption of a new identity

Extensive comorbidity/multiple diagnoses, which may include addictions, mood disorders, and personality disorders

Suicidal ideation:

- Talk about suicide
- Wish they were dead
- Have a plan to end their life

—Trauma Recovery Associates, http://www.traumarecoveryassociates
.com/signs-of-unresolved-trauma.html

Using This Book

This book is intended to introduce core concepts of recovery from trauma in the context of a survivor's practice of prayer and spirituality. It will also be helpful for people living or working with trauma survivors (who may not identify themselves as such). Healing from trauma is a long process, even for healthy people, and requires patience, gentleness, understanding, and compassion.

This book is not intended for praying in one sitting, but to serve as a prayerful guide to recovery and healing. The themes may be new or surprising or even upsetting. Some readers may experience the contents as jarring and yet liberating.

The volume is designed for extended prayer (reflection), increasing awareness (illumination), and then practicing new ways to think, feel, and behave (purification), into a healthier human being who was made in the image and likeness of God (deification). As Irenaeus tells us, "The glory of God is a human being fully alive."

A pattern might be to start with the opening prayer, read one section, reflect on the experience in one's own life, take some quiet time to listen to what God has to say about what you read and reflected on, and then end with one of the closing prayers.

Opening Prayer

Creator God, you showed your generous love
by giving Jesus to the human race.
Then you created me,
a marvelous mystery, a wonder to behold.
You understand my pain
because Jesus also suffered.
Now I present myself to you as one of your created ones,
but one who has been grievously injured.
I ask for an abundance of your healing love,
so that I may be restored to a fullness of health,
in my body, in my mind, and in my spirit.
I offer this prayer in the power of your Spirit,
through Christ our risen Lord. Amen.

—Trauma Recovery Associates, 2003

1

Jesus Enters Jerusalem

Scripture

When they drew near Jerusalem and came to Bethphage on the Mount of Olives, Jesus sent two disciples, saying to them, "Go into the village opposite you, and immediately you will find an ass tethered, and a colt with her. Untie them and bring them here to me. . . ." The disciples went and did as Jesus had ordered them. They brought the ass and the colt and laid their cloaks over them, and he sat upon them. The very large crowd spread their cloaks on the road, while others cut branches from the trees and strewed them on the road. The crowds preceding him and those following kept crying out and saying:

"Hosanna to the Son of David;
    blessed is he who comes in the name of the Lord;
hosanna in the highest." (Matt 21:1-2, 6-9)

Reflections

It was a triumphant day of excitement and joy when Jesus and his disciples entered Jerusalem. People there acclaimed him as the Son of David. Was he able to forget the people who had clashed with him or walked away? Was it a moment that he could simply enjoy without the burden of the past or worrying about the future?

Jesus was a man who showed a wide variety of emotions throughout his public ministry. He wept when he heard about the death of his friend Lazarus; he was angry toward the Pharisees and the vendors in the temple; he showed compassion to the sinful woman dragged before him in shame; he celebrated with his friends at the wedding in Cana; he enjoyed close friendships with Martha, Mary, Lazarus, and his disciple John; and he also felt the pain of betrayal by one friend and desertion by others. Jesus showed us that part of being human is to show our feelings.

However, when people have experienced trauma, they have a difficult time managing their emotions. Trauma survivors usually do not stay grounded in the present moment when they encounter emotional experiences that remind them of their hurtful past. They fear that they will not be able to tolerate their feelings in the present moment. Some may experience intense emotions when triggered by hurtful memories. They may shut down their logical thinking and can get lost in their emotions. Others deal with their emotions and triggers by numbing their feelings and relying only on their thinking.

When survivors learn to stay grounded, they are able to process their experiences and react in proportion to their situations in the present moment. And like Jesus, they are able to experience a variety of feelings with a wide range of emotional intensity.

Prayer

God, grant me the gift of healing so that I may be able to live a grounded life. Help me to enjoy the good things that are part of my life, and also to feel the human emotions that come with difficulties and distress. Help me to understand and believe that my feelings will not destroy me, but are a part of my humanity, and truly a gift from you.

2

Jesus Teaches His Disciples at the Last Supper

Scripture

[Jesus said,] "I have told you this while I am with you. The Advocate, the holy Spirit that the Father will send in my name—he will teach you everything and remind you of all that I told you. Peace I leave with you; my peace I give to you. Not as the world gives do I give it to you. Do not let your hearts be troubled or afraid. You heard me tell you, 'I am going away and I will come back to you.' If you loved me, you would rejoice that I am going to the Father; for the Father is greater than I. And now I have told you this before it happens, so that when it happens you may believe." (John 14:25-29)

Reflections

As Jesus sat with his disciples in the upper room, it appears that their hearts were overwhelmed with pain and confusion. He told them this would be their last Passover. He let them know he was moving on, and they would not be going with him. They were angry and confused and afraid. Jesus tried one more time to teach them, telling them to love one another in the way that he had loved all of them. And then he made that wonderful promise to send his Spirit who would continue to teach them, so they could remember and understand everything that he had already done.

When survivors of trauma are triggered by their memories of the past, they often react without considering their response in a thoughtful manner. They become confused because they do not understand themselves and their own choices. Sometimes they "know the right thing to do," but then they do something else, consciously or impetuously, and that leads to more heartache.

They try to "understand the world and how it works." They attempt to find ways to live that reduce their risks and help them to feel safe. But their conclusions are skewed because they are based on the circumstances related to their childhood trauma. They were caught in a harmful situation, and powerless to escape their dangerous predicament.

Prayer

Help me, God, as I live in a dark fog of mixed feelings and desires. Help me to understand the great confusion of emotions that I experienced during my trauma, and ever since then, which were simply normal reactions to what was going on in my life. Help me to find a way through the confusion and complexity of all my thoughts and feelings. Help me to hold on to a thread of hope that I can do more than merely survive my pain. Help me to believe that life can be better, and that my efforts are worthwhile.

3

Jesus Washes the Feet
of His Disciples

Scripture

[Jesus] rose from supper and took off his outer garments. He took a towel and tied it around his waist. Then he poured water into a basin and began to wash the disciples' feet and dry them with the towel around his waist. He came to Simon Peter, who said to him, "Master, are you going to wash my feet?" Jesus answered and said to him, "What I am doing, you do not understand now, but you will understand later." Peter said to him, "You will never wash my feet." Jesus answered him, "Unless I wash you, you will have no inheritance with me." Simon Peter said to him, "Master, then not only my feet, but my hands and head as well." . . . So when he had washed their feet [and] put his garments back on and reclined at table again, he said to them, "Do you realize what I have done for you? You call me 'teacher' and 'master,' and rightly so, for indeed I am. If I, therefore, the master and teacher, have washed your feet, you ought to wash one another's feet. I have given you a model to follow, so that as I have done for you, you should also do." (John 13:4-9, 12-15)

Reflections

Jesus wanted to do this last act of kindness for his closest friends, to show them how much he loved them and how close he felt to them, even in those last hours of his life. But his friend Peter—he just couldn't handle it. He felt so unworthy, and then all his awkwardness and bluster just came gushing out, as he tried to avoid the intense feelings that filled the room.

As a way to survive, trauma victims do their best to avoid their emotions, afraid of the consequences if they let their emotions surface. Consciously and unconsciously they learn a variety of thoughts and behaviors that help them to avoid their feelings. However, there are skills they can learn that will help them to regulate their uncomfortable emotions, and the anxiety that accompanies their attempts to make any changes in their lives. They can learn to correct their distorted thinking, to calm their bodies when stressed, and to integrate all of their emotions in order to decrease their intensity.

Prayer

Lord, I am not worthy—you know that better than anyone. There are so many ways that I have messed up my life. Can I ever trust you or anyone else? And how can I let myself feel my emotions when doing so has caused so many problems in the past? Help me to learn how to trust again. Help me to feel safer in the world. Help me to learn ways to protect myself in a reasonable manner, so that I can be more open to the world around me, and enjoy its many pleasures.

4

Peter Promises to Be Faithful to Jesus

Scripture

Jesus said to them, "This night all of you will have your faith in me shaken, for it is written:

'I will strike the shepherd,
  and the sheep of the flock will be dispersed';

but after I have been raised up, I shall go before you to Galilee." Peter said to him in reply, "Though all may have their faith in you shaken, mine will never be." Jesus said to him, "Amen, I say to you, this very night before the cock crows, you will deny me three times." Peter said to him, "Even though I should have to die with you, I will not deny you." And all the disciples spoke likewise. (Matt 26:31-35)

Reflections

Children are caught in a dynamic of *ambivalent attachment* when their trauma occurred. During their childhood, they naturally need relationships in which they feel safe and cared for. They also quite naturally need to avoid or escape any situation in which they are being hurt or did not feel safe. In their situations of abuse or neglect they were caught in a terrible predicament—the people they needed to care for them and keep them safe were also harming them or failing to protect them. So as children they were left with a large complex of emotions that contradicted one another—someone they loved also hurt them; someone they respected caused them harm; someone they admired did not treat them as they had a right to be treated. As children they wanted to leave, and they wanted to stay. Part of them wanted everything to change, and part of them was afraid of what change would bring.

Even when trauma occurs during adolescence or adulthood, the dynamic of ambivalent attachment remains. The people and the "rules" that should have protected them did not do so, be they friends or family, public safety officers, civil laws, government regulations, or equipment that operates properly and safely. Trauma contravenes their personal safety and, as a result, survivors feel vulnerable and powerless. And they continue to experience a great deal of confusion about whether to be close to people or be alone.

Prayer

Peter showed his own ambivalence toward you, Lord, promising to follow you and then denying you as soon as he felt threatened. In my own life I still find relationships to be difficult, with my urge to cling and my urge to keep a safe distance. Sometimes I want to run away, and sometimes I want to stay no matter what. Even my relationship with you is affected because it is hard to trust you, even though others tell me that you are good and loving. Help me to learn to trust again, so that I can feel safe when I experience the blessing of friendship and intimacy.

5

Jesus Prays in the Garden

Scripture

Then they came to a place named Gethsemane, and he said to his disciples, "Sit here while I pray." He took with him Peter, James, and John, and began to be troubled and distressed. Then he said to them, "My soul is sorrowful even to death. Remain here and keep watch." He advanced a little and fell to the ground and prayed that if it were possible the hour might pass by him; he said, "Abba, Father, all things are possible to you. Take this cup away from me, but not what I will but what you will." When he returned he found them asleep. He said to Peter, "Simon, are you asleep? Could you not keep watch for one hour? Watch and pray that you may not undergo the test. The spirit is willing but the flesh is weak." Withdrawing again, he prayed, saying the same thing. Then he returned once more and found them asleep, for they could not keep their eyes open and did not know what to answer him. He returned a third time and said to them, "Are you still sleeping and taking your rest? It is enough. The hour has come. Behold, the Son of Man is to be handed over to sinners." (Mark 14:32-41)

Reflections

How alone Jesus must have felt as he prayed in the garden. He brought along his disciples, but they couldn't even stay awake, much less give him any support in his distress. When it seemed like everything was spinning out of control, Jesus begged God to step in and save him from that horror. He prayed, but did he find any consolation in his prayer? In faith, he entrusted himself to God's way, rather than trying to manage things on his own. Still, it looked as if he had failed.

Trauma survivors try to make sense of harm they have suffered. Sometimes they come to the conclusion that God did not care about them, or that their trauma was God's will for some reason. Nothing could be further from the truth of God's love and compassion, but survivors must figure that out for themselves in their own time. Many survivors expend their efforts trying to change things that cannot be changed, and trying to influence things that are beyond their control. Their healing requires an effort to change how they think about themselves and others, about the world, and about God—it will not happen spontaneously. They must learn to trust God's providence, and God's desire for their healing no matter what has happened.

Prayer

God, grant me the serenity to accept the things I cannot change, the courage to change the things I can, and the wisdom to know the difference. Living one day at a time, enjoying one moment at a time, accepting hardship as a pathway to peace; taking, as Jesus did, the sinful world as it is, not as I would have it; trusting that you will make all things right if I surrender to your will, so that I may be reasonably happy in this life, and supremely happy with you forever in the next. Amen. (Adapted from Reinhold Niebuhr, "Serenity Prayer.")

6

Jesus Is Betrayed and His Disciples Flee

Scripture

While he was still speaking, Judas, one of the Twelve, arrived, accompanied by a large crowd, with swords and clubs, who had come from the chief priests and the elders of the people. His betrayer had arranged a sign with them, saying, "The man I shall kiss is the one; arrest him." Immediately he went over to Jesus and said, "Hail, Rabbi!" and he kissed him. Jesus answered him, "Friend, do what you have come for." Then stepping forward they laid hands on Jesus and arrested him. And behold, one of those who accompanied Jesus put his hand to his sword, drew it, and struck the high priest's servant, cutting off his ear. Then Jesus said to him, "Put your sword back into its sheath, for all who take the sword will perish by the sword. . . ." Then all the disciples left him and fled. (Matt 26:47-52, 56b)

Reflections

One of Jesus' closest disciples turned against him for his own selfish purposes. Judas turned a sign of affection upside down and made it an act of betrayal. What seemed to be an expression of love actually was an act of violent power. Thus began a horrifying series of events that led to Jesus' terrible suffering, ridicule, shame, and ultimately, his cruel death. And no one stepped forward to protect him; no one came to his rescue. His disciples and friends ran away, and he was left alone.

How appalling is it that a kiss—an expression of love—was twisted/corrupted into an act of betrayal? Many trauma survivors experienced the same kind of perversion—the persons who were in a position to care for them actually wounded them by abuse and neglect. Others caused serious harm by physical and emotional acts of violence. Others who were in a position of authority failed to protect or rescue the victims. Others who knew what was happening turned their heads and ignored the evil. Sometimes the persons who perpetrated the harm asserted their intentions were in the best interests of the victim. Others claimed they were unaware or not responsible for the neglect or abuse that were the results of their violence or carelessness.

Prayer

God, my world makes no sense. I have learned that people may say they love me and then hurt me. People may say they have my interest at heart but they are really thinking of themselves, not me. People who are supposed to protect me may do nothing to rescue me. How can I ever trust again? Lord, I need you in my life. I cannot go through this life alone; it's too painful for one person. Please help me to get past this trauma, so that I can do more than merely survive. Help me to find a satisfying life.

7

Jesus Is Put on Trial

Scripture

Those who had arrested Jesus led him away to Caiaphas the high priest, where the scribes and the elders were assembled. . . . The high priest said to him, "I order you to tell us under oath before the living God whether you are the Messiah, the Son of God." Jesus said to him in reply,

"You have said so. But I tell you:
From now on you will see 'the Son of Man
seated at the right hand of the Power'
and 'coming on the clouds of heaven.'"

Then the high priest tore his robes and said, "He has blasphemed! What further need have we of witnesses? You have now heard the blasphemy; what is your opinion?" They said in reply, "He deserves to die!". . .

When it was morning, all the chief priests and the elders of the people took counsel against Jesus to put him to death. They bound him, led him away, and handed him over to Pilate, the governor. . . . Now Jesus stood before the governor, and he questioned him, "Are you the king of the Jews?" Jesus said, "You say so." And when he was accused by the chief priests and elders, he made no answer. Then Pilate said to him, "Do you not hear how many things they are testifying against you?" But he did not answer him one word, so that the governor was greatly amazed. . . . Pilate said to them, "Then what shall I do with Jesus called Messiah?" They all said, "Let him be crucified!"

But he said, "Why? What evil has he done?" They only shouted the louder, "Let him be crucified!" (Matt 26:57, 63-66; 27:1-2, 11-14, 22-23)

Reflections

It was clear that Jesus was innocent. Witnesses did not agree about their testimony, but the trials proceeded anyway as Jesus was passed between religious and civil authorities. The justice system did not protect him. His innocence was ignored.

The people that trauma survivors should have been able to trust, the people responsible for providing protection and justice, may have failed them terribly. Maybe it was a parent or a spouse, a teacher or a friend. Perhaps they sought assistance from someone at their church, people in the social service sector, or the criminal justice system. Maybe the victims told someone, but they weren't believed; or they were told there was not enough evidence to get a conviction. And so they were victimized again.

Prayer

God, you know that, even when I sought help, I did not always receive the assistance I needed and deserved. It makes it hard for me to trust those who say they want to help me, because others failed in the past. I ask for your help so that I can learn to trust again, and not have to do everything by myself. Help me to find the good people who are trustworthy, and can give me some much-needed support and guidance.

8

Barabbas Is Freed

Scripture

But all together they shouted out, "Away with this man! Release Barabbas to us." (Now Barabbas had been imprisoned for a rebellion that had taken place in the city and for murder.) . . . So he released the man who had been imprisoned for rebellion and murder, for whom they asked, and he handed Jesus over to them to deal with as they wished. (Luke 23:18-19, 25)

Reflections

There seemed to be no question that Barabbas was guilty of a serious crime. But Pilate chose an easy way to deal with another serious issue, and so Barabbas was released and not held responsible for his offense. It's sad and unjust that Jesus was innocent and yet a guilty man was set free.

It would be a better world if all people chose their actions based on principles and values of fairness and justice. The fact is that there is evil in the world, and people make decisions for a wide variety of reasons. Some of their decisions lead to harmful consequences, and no one is completely protected from them. While people can take reasonable steps to keep themselves safe, it is unrealistic to think that anyone can live a life free from all harm or risk.

Prayer

God, you willingly became flesh and chose to live among us, knowing that you would be exposed to potential harm at others' hands. Despite your love and the wonder of your miracles, some people felt threatened and afraid of you and what you taught. And so they attacked you, and some even sought to end your life, despite your innocence. I ask for your help to live as well as I can, and not to succumb to temptation. And I need your help to heal from the actions of others who caused me harm despite my innocence, and to forgive those who never stood up for me or took no action to protect me or rescue me from those who were evil. Do not allow me to be swallowed up by my anger and fear; help me to love others as you taught us.

9

Jesus Is Mocked and Scourged

Scripture

After [Pilate] had Jesus scourged, [he] handed him over to be crucified. The soldiers led him away inside the palace, . . . and assembled the whole cohort. They clothed him in purple and, weaving a crown of thorns, placed it on him. They began to salute him with, "Hail, King of the Jews!" and kept striking his head with a reed and spitting upon him. They knelt before him in homage. And when they had mocked him, they stripped him of the purple cloak, dressed him in his own clothes, and led him out to crucify him. (Mark 15:15b-20)

Reflections

Jesus' body was mistreated and his emotions were discounted. He was treated in ways that he had never deserved. He was degraded and publicly humiliated. They twisted Jesus' words and actions and used them against him. His human dignity was ignored. His suffering was founded on innocence.

Part of the continued pain and heartache of trauma survivors is the suffering that happens after the trauma is over. Triggers remind them of their hurt-filled past, and they experience the pain of that time again and again, physically and emotionally. Survivors' choices and behaviors that are a normal consequence of the harm they suffered may also lead to additional distress, ridicule, punishments, and internal pain. Sometimes their involvement in the criminal justice system results in victims being furthered victimized or blamed for the harm that was caused by others. Survivors can learn to manage the distress they experience in their bodies by using techniques to calm themselves, so as to lessen the intensity of their physical discomfort. Simple techniques of taking deeper breaths, sitting and standing up straight, relaxing tight muscles, and considering how their thinking might be distorted—all of these can help to decrease their physical and emotional distress.

Prayer

God, why must I continue to suffer? I ask for your help to live comfortably in my body—to be healed of harmful triggers that provoke my emotions and that incite me to act in ways that hurt myself and sometimes hurt others. Help me to set aside my old habits and learn new ways to deal with my physical and emotional pain.

10

Peter Denies Knowing Jesus

Scripture

Peter said to [Jesus], "Though all may have their faith in you shaken, mine will never be." Jesus said to him, "Amen, I say to you, this very night before the cock crows, you will deny me three times." Peter said to him, "Even though I should have to die with you, I will not deny you." And all the disciples spoke likewise. . . .

Now Peter was sitting outside in the courtyard. One of the maids came over to him and said, "You too were with Jesus the Galilean." But he denied it in front of everyone, saying, "I do not know what you are talking about!" As he went out to the gate, another girl saw him and said to those who were there, "This man was with Jesus the Nazorean." Again he denied it with an oath, "I do not know the man!" A little later the bystanders came over and said to Peter, "Surely you too are one of them; even your speech gives you away." At that he began to curse and to swear, "I do not know the man." And immediately a cock crowed. Then Peter remembered the word that Jesus had spoken: "Before the cock crows you will deny me three times." He went out and began to weep bitterly. (Matt 26:33-35, 69-75)

Reflections

While Peter professed his love and commitment, Jesus knew that a short time later he would deny him. Peter was filled with such a wide variety of emotions, he hardly knew what to do.

Previously he had declared Jesus to be the Messiah, and then a minute later he tried to talk him out of following God's plan. Peter professed his willingness to follow Jesus to death, and then declared that he did not even know Jesus. Yet Jesus was able to see him with the eyes of love, and did not stop loving him.

Trauma survivors are often confused by the complexity of their emotions. They may believe that they can have only one feeling about a person or situation, but their emotions are much more complicated than that. Trauma survivors must learn that they, like everyone else, can have several feelings at the same time, and sometimes contrary feelings, even about the same person or situation. They must learn to accept that reality is complex, not simple.

Prayer

Lord, I find that I am much like Peter with a lot of different feelings, and sometimes they are overwhelming. Help me through the confusion of multiple and contrary feelings, so that I may fully express what fills my heart. Help me to know and speak the truth about my life, and not conform myself to the expectations of others out of fear of what they will think about me.

11

Judas Repents and Ends His Life

Scripture

Judas, his betrayer, seeing that Jesus had been condemned, deeply regretted what he had done. He returned the thirty pieces of silver to the chief priests and elders, saying, "I have sinned in betraying innocent blood." They said, "What is that to us? Look to it yourself." Flinging the money into the temple, he departed and went off and hanged himself. (Matt 27:3-5)

Reflections

We don't know much about Judas's motivations—was it greed? anger? revenge? Is it possible he even thought he was doing the right thing? What did Jesus see in him when he was chosen as one of his closest disciples? When Judas had a change of heart, it was too late to change what he had set in motion. It seems to have led to more intense emotions—embarrassment? regret? more anger? sadness? hopelessness? Judas didn't handle his feelings well, but chose an extreme reaction by ending his own life.

We may never fully understand why some people choose to inflict trauma on other people, including the young and vulnerable. We may never fully understand why evil exists and the innocent are harmed. Perpetrators may be trying to deal with their own complex needs and feelings, and many perpetrators are themselves survivors of childhood trauma. Nevertheless, they are still responsible for their own actions and their long-lasting effects.

The dilemma for many people is their lack of skills to regulate emotions, and a lack of awareness of a range of feeling intensity and a variety of behavioral choices. Therefore, extremes in thinking, behaving, and feeling are common.

Prayer

God, much of my life is being spent picking up the pieces—not just from my childhood or other traumatic events, but all the havoc I have created since then. I feel trapped and don't think I have choices; my emotions feel dangerous and something I have to keep shoved down in order to feel safe; my thinking is distorted and other people don't understand what seems perfectly obvious to me. Please help me to find a path for my life that doesn't lead me to such extreme reactions, so that I can feel safe as I live each day.

12

Jesus Carries His Cross to Golgotha

Scripture

Then [Pilate] handed him over to them to be crucified. So they took Jesus, and carrying the cross himself he went out to what is called the Place of the Skull, in Hebrew, Golgotha. (John 19:16-17)

Reflections

Jesus was mocked and ridiculed, whipped and beaten. There was not even a pretense of a fair trial. The judicial sentence was declared: he would be put to death by crucifixion. And so Jesus was handed the instrument of his own execution and made to carry it through town. What was it like as he walked the streets of Jerusalem? Perhaps some people looked away because they did not want to see his pain, while others seized the opportunity to point fingers and have fun at his painful expense. Maybe some of the same people who had rejoiced at his arrival just a few days before were now laughing at Jesus' downfall.

It is totally unfair that innocent people are hurt, that children are traumatized, that some people take advantage of others, that blameless people are victimized. It seems to heap injury on injury when trauma survivors realize the hard work they will have to undertake in order to recover. No one else can do it for them, and most people simply have no idea what to say or do when they find out about the abuse or neglect. So the trauma continues to have adverse effects as the victims stumble their way through the steps that lead to healing. Their personal "way of the cross" may include physical and emotional healing; recovery from bad habits and crippling addictions; learning new ways to think, feel, behave, and deal with relationships; forgiveness; and grief for the losses they have suffered.

Prayer

God, although you were innocent, you were made to carry the cross that would be used to end your life. I am angry that even though I was the one who was injured, I am also the one who has to do all the hard work to get better—it is so unfair. Staying stuck in my anger doesn't really help, so give me the strength I need to do the hard work of recovery.

13

Simon of Cyrene Helps Jesus

Scripture

As they led him away they took hold of a certain Simon, a Cyrenian, who was coming in from the country; and after laying the cross on him, they made him carry it behind Jesus. (Luke 23:26)

Reflections

Already worn down by the torture, Jesus had to shoulder the burden of his cross. Despite some well-intentioned promises to follow Jesus to his death, there was no one there to help him in his last hours on this earth. He must have looked exhausted when the soldiers grabbed a bystander and forced him to carry the cross on Jesus' behalf. Simon was another innocent man compelled to do something against his will, constrained by soldiers with more power and the means to hurt him. How did he react when he was pulled in to walk the road to Jesus' execution? And how was it for Jesus that someone else had to help? Did he feel relief and gratitude? Or did he think that it was something he was supposed to do on his own?

Trauma survivors aren't the only ones who are affected by their trauma. Family, friends, and coworkers can also suffer when they are dragged into the emotional chaos and pain of the victims or their unhealthy thoughts and behavior. Or they may be overwhelmed by their own feeling of powerlessness to help the people they care about.

Some trauma survivors feel abandoned when they engage in the work of their recovery. Sometimes there are people who do step in and offer compassion and assistance to the victims, yet it goes unnoticed. Other times trauma survivors push away those who offer to help, holding some notion that recovery means they have to do the hard work alone, or that no one else can understand. And sometimes support is offered, and accepted with a grateful spirit.

Prayer

God, help me not to push away the people who can assist me. I am starting to realize that I cannot make this journey alone; I know that I need help in order to heal. I am grateful for the people in my life who have helped me, even when they cannot carry me through the whole process. I ask for your continued help, and an openness to accept the good intentions and support of others.

14

Jesus Is Crucified

Scripture

When they came to the place called the Skull, they crucified him and the criminals there, one on his right, the other on his left. (Luke 23:33)

Reflections

Jesus did nothing wrong. Others provoked his arrest, inflicted pain, and hung him on that cross. No one came to his rescue; no one protected him from the punishment imposed on him. And yet, with the perspective of time and faith, we know that something greater occurred. Because of his innocence, Jesus was able to transform these evil actions into something that had value, meaning, and, more important, redemptive power.

Those who work with trauma survivors must tread lightly when they suggest that there might be something good that comes out of the trauma. It may be heard as "the trauma was a good thing," or as a suggestion that "the perpetrator didn't do anything wrong." In fact, terrible harm was done; the abuse and neglect were seriously wrong and damaging. But through the healing process, some survivors can say that something positive also followed (which is not the same as saying the trauma was okay). And never is innocent suffering "God's will." However, God does have the power to transform survivors, so that the trauma and its effects can be catalysts for something positive and redemptive.

Prayer

God, if there is one moment in your life I can identify with, it's your crucifixion. Even if it's not true, it feels like my shame is hanging out there for everyone to see, to point their fingers at me, to blame me for the problems I'm now facing.

You know that all I'm trying to do is survive, yet there are times when I am considered a criminal, a perpetrator, or mentally ill. I make mistakes, sometimes the same ones over and over again. Help me to preserve my innocence and not to become a bad person because of my trauma. By your power, convert my pain into something good, so that at the end of my days I will know that my suffering had some value, and the world will be a better place because I have been here.

15

Jesus Is Stripped and Shamed

Scripture

[T]hey divided his garments by casting lots; then they sat down and kept watch over him there. . . . Those passing by reviled him, shaking their heads and saying, "You who would destroy the temple and rebuild it in three days, save yourself, if you are the Son of God, [and] come down from the cross!" Likewise the chief priests with the scribes and elders mocked him and said, "He saved others; he cannot save himself. So he is the king of Israel! Let him come down from the cross now, and we will believe in him. He trusted in God; let him deliver him now if he wants him. For he said, 'I am the Son of God.'" The revolutionaries who were crucified with him also kept abusing him in the same way. . . .

And about three o'clock Jesus cried out in a loud voice, "Eli, Eli, lema sabachthani?" which means, "My God, my God, why have you forsaken me?" (Matt 27:35-36, 39-44, 46).

Reflections

In front of everyone Jesus was shamed as his clothes were stripped off and he was left exposed to the world. People continued to mock him—passersby, his religious leaders, even those who were criminals being crucified nearby. He could not save himself, and he knew that God had the power to save him. But nothing happened as death crept close. In the end, he felt abandoned by God.

Trauma victims experience the horror of human vulnerability and powerlessness. Often they turn to God to save them, and are confused, angry, and deeply hurt when God does not respond to their prayer and rescue them. Many trauma survivors lose faith in God who allows such things to happen to innocent people, and it can take a long time for them to recover a sense of faith or belief in God's enduring love.

While victims have a natural tendency to blame themselves, in fact they were victims at the hands of their perpetrators. The survivors were not able to save themselves. They continue to think that the abuse and neglect is their fault, and they conclude that they are bad and unforgivable. They speak harsh and condemning words to themselves, believing that they are ruined, unlovable, and unforgivable. They feel desolate and alone in their suffering.

Prayer

God, are you there? Have you abandoned me? Will you let me know you're there, somewhere? Will my pain ever come to an end? Is it possible to "get better," or will I be disfigured forever? Please shine your light of love on me, so that I can see some glimmer of light in my darkness. Help me to feel some semblance of love, so I can begin to heal. And help me to respect myself more and be less self-degrading.

16

Jesus Forgives

Scripture

Then Jesus said, "Father, forgive them, they know not what they do." (Luke 23:34)

Reflections

During his public ministry, Jesus showed his followers the face of God's mercy by extending forgiveness. He also taught us to forgive others in the same manner as God has forgiven us, and to pray for the grace to receive and extend forgiveness. Near the end of Jesus' life, despite his innocence and all his suffering, he managed to forgive the people who had wronged him, those who had hurt him, and those who had unjustly executed him.

Forgiveness is a process of healing the burdens that are carried by the one who was hurt; it is healing for oneself, not something done for the perpetrator. Many people have mistaken ideas about what is necessary to forgive. They have false expectations about what the victim or the perpetrator must do before they are willing to extend forgiveness. Forgiveness is not giving something to the one who caused the injury, but changing one's own behaviors, emotions, and thoughts about the person who is responsible for the wound, so that the lingering effects of the injuries can fade, and the victim can move on to live a healthier and more satisfying life.

Forgiveness is not an easy process. It requires an honesty with oneself that at times may feel brutal. It requires making a distinction between one's own responsibility and what is the responsibility of others. It demands an honest look at the effects and consequences of one's behavior. It is not a smooth and progressive process but rather has its ups, downs, and backtracking, and it may take a long time.

Its benefits are significant and worth the effort. Forgiveness can bring relief from the snare of uncomfortable emotions; correct messy and distorted thinking about oneself, others, the world, and God; and result in more conscious and just behavior going forward.

Prayer

God, I ask for the precious gift of forgiveness—first for myself, for the harm I've done to myself.

I don't really believe that the person who harmed me deserves my forgiveness. So I'm more hesitant to ask for your grace—for the desire to forgive and to learn how to forgive. There are things I still cling to that make me feel safe and strong. I'm not sure what will happen or what I will become if I actually forgive. Will others even believe I was seriously harmed if I forgive the person who hurt me?

I will need your help so that someday I may sincerely be able to forgive those who have harmed me.

17

Mary and John Are Given to One Another's Care

Scripture

When Jesus saw his mother and the disciple there whom he loved, he said to his mother, "Woman, behold, your son." Then he said to the disciple, "Behold, your mother." And from that hour the disciple took her into his home. (John 19:26-27)

Reflections

Nearby were two people whom Jesus dearly loved, a man and a woman who found the courage to stand with him in his most painful hour. Other so-called friends ran away because they found it difficult to be witnesses to his intense suffering. Yet Jesus was not so engrossed in his own pain that it stopped him from responding compassionately to Mary and John.

Trauma survivors may feel alone in their suffering, convinced that no one has suffered like they have. They know that others have been hurt, but they still believe that they are unique in their pain. They may become self-indulgent or unwilling to accept responsibility for their actions in the present with the "explanation" that they are innocent victims. They may isolate themselves from others in order to protect themselves and feel safe in the world.

Sometimes there are special people in the lives of trauma survivors that provide a place of temporary safety, or compassion and nurturance when they are distressed. They are a special gift to be appreciated. Their comforting response makes possible a significant step toward healing.

Prayer

God, help me to find the way out of the agony I have created for myself. Do not let my world shrink so much that all I ever think about is myself, so that I become overwhelmed by my pain. Help me not to push others away when they try to listen or help me; and to be open to receive the compassion and kindness that others extend to me. Help me to remember that there are other people who are suffering, and that I can reach out to them with comfort and aid. Finally, help me to find understanding in my own heart for those who are afraid or run away from me; they may not know what they are doing or the new suffering they have inflicted.

18

Jesus Dies

Scripture

It was now about noon and darkness came over the whole land until three in the afternoon because of an eclipse of the sun. Then the veil of the temple was torn down the middle. Jesus cried out in a loud voice, "Father, into your hands I commend my spirit"; and when he had said this he breathed his last. The centurion who witnessed what had happened glorified God and said, "This man was innocent beyond doubt." When all the people who had gathered for this spectacle saw what had happened, they returned home beating their breasts. (Luke 23:44-48)

Reflections

An innocent man was put to death. The outcome of misunderstanding, lying, hatred, and persecution was the torture and crucifixion of Jesus. He had to struggle just to breathe, but his last breath was a prayer. One more time Jesus handed over his life to God. Only after the fact do we hear an official proclaim his innocence. Too late do some people beat their breasts, perhaps finally realizing their complicity in failing to speak up.

Many trauma survivors feel like something inside of them has died. If they were harmed as children, they believe that their innocence was stolen, that their childhood was taken away. If they were innocent victims later on, they say things like, "Something inside me has died. I am not the same as I used to be."

Trauma victims find it hard to believe that they are loved by God. Some of them even think of death as potential relief from their pain, not aware or not believing how much pain others will experience if they were to die.

Prayer

God, where else can I turn? It seems like no one came to my aid; no one spoke up for me; no one stepped forward to move me to safety. Anything that happened seems to have been too little and too late.

That includes you! Is it even possible for me to trust you? When I was in trouble, you did not save me. When I was being hurt, you did not come to my rescue, and so I continue to suffer even now. Can I *really* count on you, as well-meaning people tell me? I am not even sure I can pray anymore, but sometimes I try.

So please listen to my prayer! Show me your love. Help me to know that you are present now, watching over me and protecting me. Then maybe, just maybe, someday, I will be able to trust you again, and entrust my life into your hands.

19

The Body of Jesus Is Entombed

Scripture

Now there was a virtuous and righteous man named Joseph who, though he was a member of the council, had not consented to their plan of action. He came from the Jewish town of Arimathea and was awaiting the kingdom of God. He went to Pilate and asked for the body of Jesus. After he had taken the body down, he wrapped it in a linen cloth and laid him in a rock-hewn tomb in which no one had yet been buried. It was the day of preparation, and the sabbath was about to begin. The women who had come from Galilee with him followed behind, and when they had seen the tomb and the way in which his body was laid in it, they returned and prepared spices and perfumed oils. (Luke 23:50-56a)

Reflections

After all that had happened, did Jesus feel relief that he no longer felt physical or emotional pain?

Does it seem too little and too late that some people were more concerned about Jesus' body after he died than when he was cruelly treated and brutally killed? Perhaps it took courage for them to show any interest in Jesus by participating in his burial.

Trauma survivors suffer greatly when they are injured, and their injuries last for a long time. They experience more victimization when their suffering is ignored.

So many victims of violence learn how to turn off their feelings as a way to survive their pain. They believe that their emotions are uncontrollable and dangerous, and so the best thing they can do is "not feel." They miss out on much of life because they don't feel their emotions, and they pass through much of their lives feeling numb.

Prayer

God, there are days I feel like I'm done. I can't do any more, and I need to find some relief. I'm shut down, numb, dead to all feeling, unable to move. Life is moving around me but I have no desire or strength to participate. Help me to come out of my own self-created tomb of hopelessness, despair, and death. Call me out into life again, like you did for your close friend Lazarus, so that I may enjoy the good things that are a part of your creation.

20

The Disciples Grieve

Scripture

[Mary Magdalene] went and told his companions who were mourning and weeping. When they heard that he was alive and had been seen by her, they did not believe. (Mark 16:10-11)

Reflections

Jesus' disciples were overcome with grief. They had lost a dear friend and teacher. Their hopes were smashed because they had expected a different outcome, someone who would save Israel. They were also concerned about their personal safety, wondering if Jesus' followers could be the next ones arrested and killed. And so they shut themselves away, locked up with their sadness and fear.

Trauma survivors have plenty of reasons to be afraid. Despite their best efforts when they were injured, they were not able to protect themselves, and that incapacity to keep themselves safe may have continued even into adulthood. They also have good reasons to mourn, for the terrible things that happened to them, and for the things they enjoyed and then lost because of their woundedness. They also grieve for what they never had, for what should have happened and never did. They may believe that they'll never feel better or that, if they allow themselves to feel their sadness and anger, it will overwhelm them. So they may spend great amounts of energy trying to keep themselves safe, and trying to keep away the deep sadness and intense anger. While trying to preserve their lives and avoid their deep feelings, they end up losing out on much of what life has to offer.

When trauma survivors engage in a healthy process of grieving their losses, they improve their ability to hold contradictory feelings at the same time. They learn to experience sadness and anger simultaneously, a prerequisite for living a healthy life. They become more balanced and are less likely to react based on an extreme emotion or perception. The benefits of healthy grief slowly begin to emerge internally and externally.

Prayer

God, I ask for the power of your resurrection to raise me up from the valley of death. I need your healing power to work within me, to bring me consolation, relief, and peace as I experience my grief. I want your help to learn ways to protect myself and feel safe without completely blocking out the world. I need your help to let myself feel the intense emotions that come whenever I think about what I have lost and what I never had. Help me to grieve all the damage that has occurred as a result of my trauma—my childhood, my family, my broken relationships, my self-esteem and personal power, my health, and my trust in you. Lead me on a safe path toward the fullness of life that you want for all of us.

21

Jesus Is Raised from Death

Scripture

On the first day of the week, Mary of Magdala came to the tomb early in the morning, while it was still dark, and saw the stone removed from the tomb. So she ran and went to Simon Peter and to the other disciple whom Jesus loved, and told them, "They have taken the Lord from the tomb, and we don't know where they put him." So Peter and the other disciple went out and came to the tomb. They both ran, but the other disciple ran faster than Peter and arrived at the tomb first; he bent down and saw the burial cloths there, but did not go in. When Simon Peter arrived after him, he went into the tomb and saw the burial cloths there, and the cloth that had covered his head, not with the burial cloths but rolled up in a separate place. Then the other disciple also went in, the one who had arrived at the tomb first, and he saw and believed. For they did not yet understand the scripture that he had to rise from the dead. Then the disciples returned home. (John 20:1-10)

Reflections

Jesus' human life had been transformed, but the disciples were unaware. All they saw was an empty tomb. How could they explain this—to themselves or to others? Maybe they went home because they didn't know what else to do.

Like the tomb on Easter morning, emptiness can be a fact or it can be a feeling. It's a natural human desire to look for an explanation, to search for meaning, especially when something has caused us confusion and pain. Yet how can anyone think that a life-changing trauma could be meaningful or have a purpose?

That is the paradox and the joy of Jesus' death and resurrection—a horror has become our salvation. The mystery of the cross coexists with the glory of the empty tomb. Together they point to the truth that there is a path through tragedy and victimization. God can take human suffering and absurdity and meaninglessness and transform them into something good.

Prayer

God, you raised Jesus from the dead, and that was unbelievable. Is it really possible that something good could emerge from my trauma? That also seems unbelievable, even cruel to suggest. So I dare to ask you again for your resurrecting power to raise me up from the valley of death. With an unconvinced heart, I ask for your divine wisdom, that someday I might find a meaning to my trauma. In the meantime, I ask for your grace-filled presence and your strength to persevere in all that lies ahead in my life.

22

The Risen Jesus Appears to the Women at His Tomb

Scripture

After the sabbath, as the first day of the week was dawning, Mary Magdalene and the other Mary came to see the tomb. And behold, there was a great earthquake; for an angel of the Lord descended from heaven, approached, rolled back the stone, and sat upon it. His appearance was like lightning and his clothing was white as snow. The guards were shaken with fear of him and became like dead men. Then the angel said to the women in reply, "Do not be afraid! I know that you are seeking Jesus the crucified. He is not here, for he has been raised just as he said. Come and see the place where he lay. Then go quickly and tell his disciples, 'He has been raised from the dead, and he is going before you to Galilee; there you will see him.' Behold, I have told you." Then they went away quickly from the tomb, fearful yet overjoyed, and ran to announce this to his disciples. And behold, Jesus met them on their way and greeted them. They approached, embraced his feet, and did him homage. (Matt 28:1-9)

Reflections

Although Jesus had told them he would be raised from the dead, his disciples did not understand. How could they imagine such a thing that had never been seen before? And yet Jesus had raised the widow's son at Nain, and the young daughter of Jairus. Most spectacularly, he had raised Lazarus after he had been in the tomb for days. As he told Martha and Mary, he *is* resurrection and life. Death cannot maintain any hold on him. And he asks us to believe the same—that united with him, there is resurrection after death.

Despite its serious and long-lasting effects, trauma is not the end of life. There can be new life, even after the devastation of abuse and neglect. Hard as it is to believe, there can be satisfaction, and fulfillment, and peace.

Prayer

God, your promise is almost too much to believe. Is it really possible, after all I have been through, that I can have some peace? Is it really possible that I can feel alive and safe at the same time? Help me to believe that what the women saw was true. And help me to believe that their good news was not just for them but also for me—that despite all my darkness, there can also be light; that despite all my fear, there can be hope; that despite my emptiness, I can be filled again. Do not leave me alone in my tomb!

23

The Risen Jesus Appears
to More Disciples

Scripture

On the evening of that first day of the week, when the doors were locked, where the disciples were, for fear of the Jews, Jesus came and stood in their midst and said to them, "Peace be with you." When he had said this, he showed them his hands and his side. The disciples rejoiced when they saw the Lord. [Jesus] said to them again, "Peace be with you. . . ."

Now a week later his disciples were again inside and Thomas was with them. Jesus came, although the doors were locked, and stood in their midst and said, "Peace be with you." Then he said to Thomas, "Put your finger here and see my hands, and bring your hand and put it into my side, and do not be unbelieving, but believe." Thomas answered and said to him, "My Lord and my God!" (John 20:19-21, 26-28)

Reflections

Jesus' disciples had abandoned him in his time of greatest need, and yet he returned to them and offered to them his gift of peace. He did not hide himself because he had been beaten down and executed. He was able to show them the nail holes in his hands and feet, and the opening in his side caused by a soldier's lance. Jesus was not held captive by shame although he had died. His wounds were in fact a sign that God's life in him had transformed him.

Most trauma survivors are unwilling to reveal their wounds and their scars. They are afraid that, if people find out about their history, their relationships will end because people will believe they were bad, and so they hide in shame. They hold the erroneous belief that the trauma was *their own* fault, rather than the misbehavior of a perpetrator or the failure of another person to act. Trauma victims must learn the truth: that their childhood trauma does not negate their goodness. They must also learn how to remember their injuries and see things that remind them of their past without being swept away in shame or trying to numb their feelings. Living with their scars is a sign of their victory, not a sign of defeat.

Prayer

God, you know me through and through, despite my attempts to hide myself from you. (This behavior goes as far back as Adam and Eve trying to hide themselves in shame.) Help me to be more open in my prayer, to be my real self in your presence. May your healing power transform my shame into self-confidence, and my belief that "I am bad" into the realization that I am lovable. May I grow in gratitude for what you have done for me.

24

The Risen Jesus Converses
with Two Disciples

Scripture

Now that very day two of them were going to a village seven
miles from Jerusalem called Emmaus, and they were conversing
about all the things that had occurred. And it happened that
while they were conversing and debating, Jesus himself drew
near and walked with them, but their eyes were prevented from
recognizing him. He asked them, "What are you discussing as
you walk along?" They stopped, looking downcast. One of them,
named Cleopas, said to him in reply, "Are you the only visitor
to Jerusalem who does not know of the things that have taken
place there in these days?" And he replied to them, "What sort
of things?" They said to him, "The things that happened to Jesus
the Nazarene, who was a prophet mighty in deed and word
before God and all the people, how our chief priests and rulers
both handed him over to a sentence of death and crucified him.
But we were hoping that he would be the one to redeem Israel;
and besides all this, it is now the third day since this took place.
Some women from our group, however, have astounded us:
they were at the tomb early in the morning and did not find his
body; they came back and reported that they had indeed seen a
vision of angels who announced that he was alive. Then some
of those with us went to the tomb and found things just as the
women had described, but him they did not see." And he said
to them, "Oh, how foolish you are! How slow of heart to believe

all that the prophets spoke! Was it not necessary that the Messiah should suffer these things and enter into his glory?" Then beginning with Moses and all the prophets, he interpreted to them what referred to him in all the scriptures. (Luke 24:13-27)

Reflections

The two disciples could not make sense of the news they had received. Their expectations clashed with what they were hearing, and their emotions were tangled because their hopes had been dashed. The result was distorted thinking and confused feelings, rather than being fully present to what was occurring right before their own eyes. Jesus helped them to see and understand what the Scriptures said and how they referred to his life and death.

One common effect of any traumatic event is distorted thinking. The traumatic event itself makes no sense, yet it's natural to search for meaning in the significant events of our lives. The conclusions drawn by trauma survivors will be skewed because the original situation was so "out of order." Yet the survivors will more often than not hold on to their conclusions rather than evaluate and correct them as they grow older. Applying their old safety rules and perceptions from the past to new situations in the present can be a recipe for misery and misfortune.

Prayer

God, I know that I need your healing power—not just for physical and emotional healing, but also for healing my mind. My messy thinking and my inaccurate assumptions and conclusions continue to interfere and wreak havoc in my life. Help me to think clearly so that my feelings and behavior are reasonable responses to what is happening now, and not simply reactions to what happened in my past.

25

Peter Encounters Jesus at the Beach

Scripture

When they had finished breakfast, Jesus said to Simon Peter, "Simon, son of John, do you love me more than these?" He said to him, "Yes, Lord, you know that I love you." He said to him, "Feed my lambs." He then said to him a second time, "Simon, son of John, do you love me?" He said to him, "Yes, Lord, you know that I love you." He said to him, "Tend my sheep." He said to him the third time, "Simon, son of John, do you love me?" Peter was distressed that he had said to him a third time, "Do you love me?" and he said to him, "Lord, you know everything; you know that I love you." [Jesus] said to him, "Feed my sheep. Amen, amen, I say to you, when you were younger, you used to dress yourself and go where you wanted; but when you grow old, you will stretch out your hands, and someone else will dress you and lead you where you do not want to go." (John 21:15-18)

Reflections

Peter was one of Jesus' more impetuous disciples, and he often showed his feelings quite openly. But other times his attempts to avoid discomfort also caused him difficulties. Jesus knew his guilt about denying his relationship with him, and gave him this opportunity to reaffirm his love for Jesus. Then he went on to tell him that not everything in our life is under our control. Even when we love, even when we love deeply, there's no guarantee that everything will turn out perfect—it didn't for Jesus, and it won't for us. Jesus called Peter back to one simple principle—love.

Some trauma survivors believe that recovery means everything will become perfect, or that everything will return to "the way it would have been if there had been no trauma." The truth is that innocent victims cannot rearrange the past in order to restore their innocence; they can move forward only into the future. Trauma survivors can learn to love again, and they can love generously and intensely. They must remember that no one is able to control everything in their lives; people can respond as best as they can with only whatever skills they possess.

Prayer

God, you know that I want to love you, and how I also hesitate and find it difficult. Despite my imperfections and failures, I ask that you continue to give me freedom to learn and to grow. I need your help to be relieved of my anxiety and my desire to control the world around me. Please give me more time so that I can do better and love more.

26

Jesus Ascends to God

Scripture

The eleven disciples went to Galilee, to the mountain to which Jesus had ordered them. When they saw him, they worshiped, but they doubted. Then Jesus approached and said to them, "All power in heaven and on earth has been given to me. Go, therefore, and make disciples of all nations, baptizing them in the name of the Father, and of the Son, and of the holy Spirit, teaching them to observe all that I have commanded you. And behold, I am with you always, until the end of the age." (Matt 28:16-20)

Reflections

The disciples came to the mountain as they had been instructed to do; and yet, after all that they had seen and heard, they still doubted. Their ambivalence continued, and maybe that's just part of being human. Nevertheless, imperfect as they were, Jesus entrusted them with the great responsibility of carrying his message to the whole world. And Jesus assured them of his abiding presence to the end—that he will never abandon his disciples or make them "go it alone."

People who have been traumatized often feel as though they are cut off and "on their own," because the people they had counted on to protect them and take care of them failed in that responsibility. Life can feel very precarious when trust becomes skewed—be it trusting too much or not trusting at all. Trauma survivors must take the risk to come out of their locked rooms and deal with life as it is. They have to learn to handle the triggers that remind them of their past hurts rather than avoid anything that provokes uncomfortable feelings. Over time they must assimilate the wide variety of their experiences—in a world that encompasses beauty and ugliness, sweetness and bitterness, beautiful music and harsh noise—as well as the broad range of their emotions, including sorrow and joy, fear and courage, anger and peace.

Prayer

God, I have heard the promise made by Jesus whom you raised from the dead—that he will always be with me. With Christ on my side, I believe that I can handle whatever comes my way—sometimes well and sometimes not so well. I can respond appropriately when I am triggered; I can choose suitable responses when my emotions are high; I can seek help instead of trying to do everything by myself; I can accept that life is complicated and not as tidy as I would like.

I know now that I have the strength not only to survive but to thrive abundantly until the day I join you in eternal life.

27

The Disciples Receive
the Spirit of Jesus

Scripture

On the evening of that first day of the week, when the doors were locked, where the disciples were, for fear of the Jews, Jesus came and stood in their midst and said to them, "Peace be with you." When he had said this, he showed them his hands and his side. The disciples rejoiced when they saw the Lord. [Jesus] said to them again, "Peace be with you. As the Father has sent me, so I send you." And when he had said this, he breathed on them and said to them, "Receive the holy Spirit. Whose sins you forgive are forgiven them, and whose sins you retain are retained." (John 20:19-23)

Reflections

Jesus couldn't help himself, could he? No matter how much he had given, he gave more. He had already handed over his life, although he had nothing to gain by that personally. After the resurrection Jesus returned to his grieving disciples and showed them his compassionate heart, granting them his peace, and demonstrating once again his message of forgiveness. As they learned Jesus' commandment to love one another, they also had to learn to forgive.

The recovery of trauma survivors need not remain private. They can learn there is no need to hide because they have no reason to be ashamed. Through their suffering and their healing, they have significant things to share with the world—their experiences of survival, resilience, formation, grieving, and forgiveness. They can be at peace with themselves, other people, the world around them, and even the one who was responsible for their trauma.

This is all possible through the great consolation and healing power of the Holy Spirit. The Consoler is the one who comes to "be with the one who was alone." The Healer promises and guides and fulfills God's desire for our wholeness and our holiness. Trauma survivors can invite the Healing Consoler to enter them and then receive God's transformative gifts.

Prayer

Come, Holy Spirit! Come, and do not delay! Bring your passionate love into my body, mind, and spirit. Do as Jesus promised and make your dwelling place within me. Blow, you mighty wind! Burn, you purifying fire! Grant me the gifts of your healing and consolation, so I might be recreated. Come with your transforming power, so that I can stand strong in the honest truth of my own experience. Grant me the courage to give clear witness to your healing power, so that together we can renew the face of the earth.

Closing Prayers

Prayer to the Holy Spirit

Come Holy Spirit, descend from God,
And make your presence known to us.

Holy Spirit, be our guest,
Make your dwelling place in us.

Fill our emptiness, give us rest,
Console us in our heart's distress.

Enlighten our darkness, forgive our sins,
And guide us when we start to stray.

Bend the rigid, melt the frozen,
Rain softly on the dry and brittle.

Allay the gloom, warm the chill,
Heal all wounds and renew our life.

Give us the promised reward of virtue:
Salvation, eternal life, and joy that never ends.

Amen! Alleluia!

Magnificat

Mary's prayer following the annunciation of her pregnancy can be an appropriate prayer for trauma survivors. Her prayer is a faith-filled and hopeful response to her "humiliation" (v. 48); and the root word for "lowly" (v. 52) can suggest those who have been abused or violated in any way:

And Mary said: My soul proclaims the greatness of the Lord
and my spirit rejoices in God my Savior;
because he has looked upon the humiliation of his servant.
Yes, from now onwards all generations will call me blessed,
for the Almighty has done great things for me.
Holy is his name,
and his faithful love extends age after age to those
who fear him.
He has used the power of his arm, he has routed the
arrogant of heart.
He has pulled down princes from their thrones and
raised high the lowly.
He has filled the starving with good things, sent the
rich away empty.
He has come to the help of Israel his servant,
mindful of his faithful love
—according to the promise he made to his ancestors—of his
mercy to Abraham and to his descendants for ever.

—Luke 1:46-55, New Jerusalem Bible